Paul Smart and Richard Kroehling

A Covid Waltz
In Words & Images WITH
DIFFERENT
EYES

Barrytown, NY

"…a near View of Death would reconcile Men of good
Principles one to another, and that it is chiefly owing to our
easy Scituation in Life, and putting these Things far
from us, that our Breaches are formented, ill Blood
continued, Prejudices, Breach of Chanimosities among us,
and bring us to see with differing Eyes, than those which
we look'd on Things with before."

—Daniel Defoe, *A Journal of the Plague Year*

"I'd like very much to make a confident picture.
I would like to be as good as nature, which, with a shower,
produces flowers and grass to cover the destruction.
But we are surrounded by human fragmentation,
by pessimism, and it is difficult to talk of other things."

—Federico Fellini

F**ebruary 2020.** This started as a story about fashion. Milan Fashion Week Emerging Talents Runway Show. Leopard-skin lederhosen, flowing furs, high-end street chic.

An Asian family in masks in the airport when we flew to Madrid. No masks or medical protocols at JFK on our way back to Albany, New York, where we live.

Our son coughed through the trip. He vomited at school the morning after we flew in. My wife stayed home to nurse him for two days. I charged back into work, figuring my malaise was just jet lag.

Then I collapsed. Aches, pains, a headache and complete exhaustion; it was all I could do to get out of bed. Breathing labored; throat so sore I couldn't speak.

Fawn called my doctor.

"We recently returned from Milan."

"Go to Emergency Room."

"Now?"

"Yes, now. The whole family."

They mask me. Rush me into quarantine. Put me on a gurney. Roll me down emptied-out halls to an examination room packed with equipment. Doctors, nurses and hospital staff in surgical masks and plastic visors watch me from afar.

"Protocol," a nurse says.

Swabs stuck up each nostril.

"You'll be out in no time," a doc says.

"I hope so."

I gag as my throat is probed.

"If you do test positive for coronavirus, they'll have to quarantine your whole family, including the cats and dog."

"Call me the Corona Angel." The nurse curtsies. She wears mismatched cloth gowns and paper pantaloons. Plastic coverings on her feet; rubberized gloves. A shower cap, mask and face shield.

I take a photo. My wife and kid post it.

Home. Still sick. The doctor says influenza. Some type not covered by the previous autumn's shots. He prescribes an inhaler, a Z-Pack. Liquids and sleep. Each cough hurts. Foul-tasting brownish gunk from deep in my lungs. I treasure my cool bedroom with its tall ceilings, marble fireplace, heirloom furniture. I play melancholic music. I read, I write.

I look up *thanatophobia,* fear of death or anxiety around death, becoming pathological if it becomes a preoccupation, as has been known to happen during times of plague or war. Slippery wormhole backed by adagios. Waltzing Matilda, played real slow. "Once a jolly swagman camped by a billabong...You'll come a-waltzing Matilda, with me."

A pair of stories about my Covid scare are published in one of the newspapers I work for. "I feel cozy when sick," I write. "I try to stare mortality down," I write. How's that working out for what you like to think of as your jaundiced journalist's outlook? Eyes won't cry. "Reports on the illness sweep across Asia and Europe. Now spiking in New York City."

My readers just want to know if I caught the disease or not.

It turns out I was never officially given the coronavirus test. I'm told to call the county Department of Health.

"As long as you're getting better, just stay at home and try not to expose people."

Expose them to what?

Nurse Mary stops by the house daily. Drops off wipes, hand sanitizer, scratchy industrial-weight tissues. Northern Italy shuts down. My wife is living on the couch.

"There's a lot of gray," nurse Mary says. "People want black and white." It seems to me that death is pretty black and white.

Both my parents recently died. There was nothing gray about it. It was black and white, and I would say it was mostly black. The jolly swagman didn't feel like mincing steps. He was no waltzing bear.

My mother fought cancer until she didn't.

My dad reread books he loved (the Russians, of course) and looked out the window. Had his martini, rocks, each day at 6:00 p.m. sharp.

My parents, apart for over forty years.

I'd call my mother often during her radiation and chemo. I stopped in at her alma mater, Oberlin College, while chaperoning my son's class on a trip to Detroit and Chicago. Called her and promised we'd get her back there.

Did the same thing in Seattle a couple of months later. Sent photos from the hospital where I, her oldest, was born. The house where we lived in a third-floor walk-up.

It feels like a lifetime ago. It is a lifetime ago.

My godfather, after whom I'm named, grew ill at the time of my mother's memorial service. I visited him in hospital. He slipped into dementia and died. We attended his funeral in place of my father, the two having grown estranged following a decades-long friendship that included adultery. Another child.

My sister and I called dad as we drove down to mom's house, which we were closing up and selling. He asked about Paul's funeral. Was more silent than usual, choosing for once not to interpret with his own experiences.

My father died a fortnight later.

I curl into my darkness. There's birdsong outside.

I **get offered money** to blog about the lockdown. Europe shuttered. NYC and California numbers soar. Restaurants stop serving. The library where I work closes. So do schools. So does the print newspaper I write for. I blog.

Item one: Take my son and dog for a drive. Playgrounds cordoned with police tape. Dog, off leash, skittering through an abandoned factory. Broken ice on the river.

My wife's snippish at home.

"It's never going to be the same," she says, complaint in counterpoint to the sleet snapping at our kitchen window. Winter darkness feeling ominous this close to spring, as if it will never cease.

We had rocky years before we moved to our raucous neighborhood in downtown Albany. Went through six therapists, two before our son entered our lives. The rest in response to his obstinate ways.

I wonder how things'll hold up through whatever it is that's descended upon us. Is our house big enough?

Will we pull closer together or drift back apart? Fight-or-flight. What is the effect of having narcissistic, needy parents? A jolly swagman. A mincing bear.

"If we hold the flame right we'll pull together and a new world will be birthed." Second blog. My library friend Regina speed talked, describing a 600-person Zoom with fellow Sufis. Hafiz: *The music tonight is love.*

Really? Regina called to cure her loneliness.

One week into lockdown.

"I suffered from despair and sleepless angst," she says. "I'd remind myself of the monks who pray for our safety and healing."

Guess it can't hurt.

How are we all going to come out of this?

It's eerily quiet. No cars. No sirens. A heavy spring snow begins to fall.

You gauge where you can drive when roads grow slick. Find the best-plowed routes. Spin out a few times; learn to decline Palmer Hill, Echo Notch, Highmount.

Gauging risk, as we're all doing now.

My mother saw our Albany home before we bought it. No electricity, but she could appreciate why we asked her to bridge costs as we waited to sell our old house.

I showed her photos on my phone's small screen.

"It looks beautiful, Paul," she said, in bed. "I need to rest now, love."

Dad came up the Christmas after mom's death. My sister and her kids. We put him and his wife up in the

State Street Hilton. Couldn't make it upstairs to see our bedrooms but enjoyed what he saw.

I made him his martini, sat him in my reading chair. He eyes the room. Comments on things that were his through various relationships. Always the English professor. Arbiter of taste, dictator of feelings.

He increasingly repeated one story as he aged: How he shut himself into the apartment closet where his single mother would hang her coat after work every day. He'd get her attention. But it was warm that day.

"My damage started there," he'd proclaim, proudly.

I bang on the window. Squirrels. They look back, unmoved. My cats track them from window to window. Wind tosses the backyard evergreens. The doorbell rings and I scamper.

A masked postal worker waves from across the street. I pick up my packages from within the stoop's snow-covered milk box. There's a spot in the curbside gravel where snow isn't sticking. The pink embryo of a bird. Sad, yes? Is it sad? *Whose is that jumbuck you've got in your tucker bag?*

I listen to wind. Distant sirens.

M-A-G-N-I-F-I-C-A-T-I-O-N.

Bereaved. Bereavement. The state of loss versus the acts described by grief. Dantean realms of hospitals and hospice. So caring. So hopeless. Mortuary arrangements and obligatory services. Expectations of how one should react. Or not.

"Coping ugly" was how one pioneer in the field once put it.

Death is the mother of beauty. No solace. *Reave.*
Reaving. Be-reaved.

The robbing of a person of something both abstract
and tactile. Robbed by force.

My sister spent the time between our parents' passing and Covid
by visiting close friends of our dead. I, like my wife when her mother
died, feel relieved. Able to live our lives for ourselves. We have shifted
our view of family inward.

Transformation. The recognition of a life's treasures. The unde-
niable fact that most is just junk. My wife and I talk about cleaning
house.

The snows melt fast. People are pulling weeds from the edges of their
yards. Forsythias bloom. Daffodils!

"We're all in this together," reads a sign on a shuttered business.
I take my son on a drive around the city. Quiet streets. Empty side-
walks. Only the local convenience stores stayed open.

The emptiness is striking enough to pull my son from his phone.
He asks about the age of buildings. Why some seem noble while others are left to rot.

"Did you get a game in before they took the hoops down?"

He shrugs.

"We're playing online."

I ask if he wants to explore beyond the city.

He gives it some thought. "Let's take the dog. We'll get lunch."

The remnants of the Erie Canal. We parallel the Mohawk River for an
hour. Get off the Thruway at Little Falls, a former mill town, and spot
an empty lock where there are info kiosks. Let the dog loose. Watch a
group of young people scale a stone wall, then rappel back down.

We grab a drive-thru lunch. Zigzag through town. Something stripped the place of its soul long ago.

We feed Berry, our Cattle Dog mix in the back seat, chicken nuggets when they cool.

I play classics on the way out: Beatles, Marvin, Coltrane. Milo feeds his playlist into the system as we return east. I try rapping.

"Stop. Just stop."

He hits pause. Stares me down.

Sun beams splay the road before us, our car's shadow lengthening into the gold. The river shimmers to our left.

"The silence is nice, Dad. Let's do this again."

Like balm. I could die happy.

"Will it be a normal summer?"

The boy has been inside, except for our father-son drives, for weeks.

"Will my friends and I be able to hang out?"

"I don't know."

Camps are canceled. Not that our son ever liked camp.

I itch to have my antibodies tested. I feel every Covid symptom I read about. I watch the market and my money slip.

I no longer know what to read. I want to get lost in a narrative that interrupts the world we have entered. James isn't right, neither is Tolstoy, Dickens or Twain. All too long-winded, too pretty. Too old. Like work. I want an escape.

I return to the wine-scented Parisian melancholy and forced introspection of Maigret. His mysteries' descriptions of working cityscapes, corner cafes, offices made homey by the warmth of a coal fire, the lighting of a pipe. A cassoulet gets served to the inspector detective at their apartment's cozy table by an attentive Mrs. Maigret.

"It just happened. As though a moment comes when it's both necessary and natural to make a decision that has long since been made."

Too bad Georges Simenon isn't alive to write about now.

I recall a storytelling night I produced at Joe's Pub. After tales of High Adventure, a petite woman who worked at the U.N. described how to shut down New York.

"Set off one landmine in Central Park," she said demurely, arms wrapping her chest. "Then announce that there's another hidden somewhere."

It was the one story I held on to from that evening two decades past, when Y2K was our biggest fear.

I talk to friends by phone. We exchange observations about how things are looking from our cozy homescapes. How long would this last?

Refuge may be the word this year. From the Latin *fugere,* to flee.

To flee deeper inside?

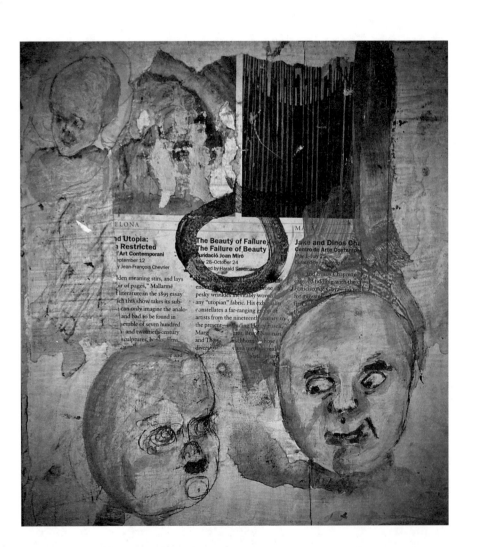

21

I lift my veil of endless deadlines. I watch spring unfold. Wind, rain, blossoms, sun. I did this years ago, before a career, before rebuilding my life around insurance and saving accounts. Before family.

I'm older than my parents were when undergoing mid-life changes. Divorces and cross-country treks. New families. More divorces. Charlottesville, Alaska, and Manhattan in-laws. Interventions. Half-sisters and even a hint, at one point, of mom and dad hooking up again. Agita.

A painter friend dies. His wife couldn't be with him as he took his last breath. I couldn't reach her to offer condolences. Wrote his obituary anyway.

My wife's in job hell. We find peace in television. Lush technicolor epics from the 50's and 60's. A bit of violence to close each hushed day: Ray Donovan, the eternal fixer. Lucy Liu as a Manhattan-based Dr. Watson. The gentle humor and truth of a quiet British series, *The Detectorists*. Reinforcements for our cozy corner.

Hours unwind. I'm up at five, awakened by the text alerts on my wife's phone.

I make lists. Lists of the lists. No lines through any of the fourteen items by noon. I could do laundry at least! Wake my teenager up!

"Will you shut your damned door!" I snipe at Fawn on her endless phone calls.

Her work. My work.

"Will you shut my door, dammit!" adds my son from his room.

Cemeteries—my go-to place. I've never gotten lost in one. I see more people than usual walking them, hands behind their backs. Because they're designed as contemplative landscapes?

The dog races wild. Sniffs the edges of fallen headstones near signs that forbid off-leash pets. Who cares now?

Will we emerge from captivity with fresh ideas? Many of us have long awaited times when our money systems would collapse. Debts would disappear. Is that what's coming?

I'm talking about death more. Searching out ways to sharpen my analysis of the darker corners of life. To balance my aging body's aches against my wife's optimism, once a Midwestern trait. My son's caustic adolescence.

St. Patty's Day's been canceled. I play The Pogues' version of 'And the Band Played Waltzing Matilda,' a 1971 anti-war take on Banjo Peterson's ode to itinerants in the Australian bush, when waltzing meant hoofing it, a Matilda was a bedroll, and most workers were swag-men, rambling job to job.

Songs of loss. Words for survival.

> **My father** made his funeral arrangements half a life-time before he passed.
>
> My sister and I never found a spot to memorialize our mother. Years of moving caught up with her. With us.

Fawn, my wife, wants a bush or tree to be remembered by. She had a spot picked out. Then we moved.

"It's Milo's decision," she says.

Milo. The boy we adopted when he was two days old.

> **I'm playing games** with fate, gauging my luck. All our destinies. I run through various forms of solitaire, one after another. I fail, I start over after a bit of writing to see if that changes things.
>
> Counting as I walk: Cracks in the sidewalk. An internal ledger of debts and assets. Pros and cons. I've even returned to an old habit learned on long rides to and from school.

I would watch rain drops on the window of the bus, or whatever car picked me up after my father decided it best for me to hitch back and forth to school. I'd choose a single raindrop and race it against others.

Now I'm doing it on the streaked window before my desk. The fate of my work, our household, depends on the outcome. This community, nation, world.

Dangerous as mercury. Coexistent hope and hopelessness.

Milo recharges his phone. He's gone, in a daze.

"What's on your mind?"

"Chasing raindrops," he says.

He sleeps into the afternoon. I envy his teen hours.

"Will you teach me to play Fortnite? Call of Duty?"

I need a restart. I'm tiring of my blog, the conversations I have with friends. My wife and I have had it with our closeness through lockdown. Nice dinners but different chairs for our teevee nights. Shared couch nights with footrubs have dropped away.

Maybe Milo has better answers, a clearer approach to these changes.

Me and the kid hadn't sat together and gamed since our last house move. I know the kids who let me in their virtual room. They've all slept over, pre-Covid. They help me pick a "skin," and I become a svelte-bodied female with a panda head and a broadsword.

"Give me the Uzi, too," I demand.

I keep getting killed.

I get cookies and milk for the boy. And me. 1:30 a.m.

"You sure you're okay?" he asks. "I don't need to wake Mommy, do I?"

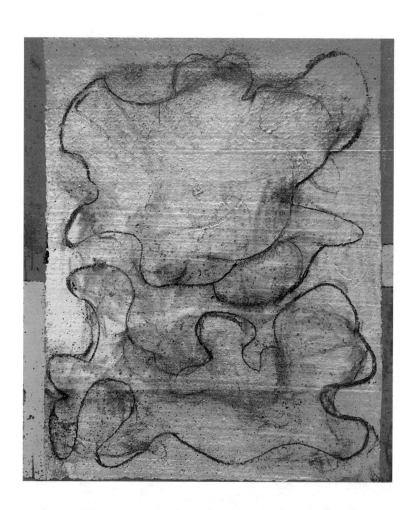

More bird embryos, nestled on the asphalt's edge. Endless Spring. Dirty blanket sky. Off rhythm.

I read the weather app: Thunderhead icons. Then cheery sun.

Blogging tempests: *I want to be rained on. Soaked. Scared sensible.*

I start looking forward to the weekly shop. We find special items in dollar stores, bodegas. Aldi's German cast-offs. Strudel, chocolate, cheese, bratwurst. Several Asian places open for takeout. We get dressed up once a week as a break from the leisure wear that's become ever-more fashionable.

Our money's fine with new help from Congress. I'm offered another daily blog. A parenting publication wants to give families a sense of hope.

Gardening time. I think of the farm school I attended. I've equated the smell of cow shit with academia ever since.

Mother was too impatient to garden. Dad hired me for a summer pulling poison ivy out of hedges.

"Burn the stuff," he told me. The smoke sent me to the emergency room.

I don't like dirt. My wife's the gardener.

Our neighborhood grime has a sense of danger. It's a breeding ground. We take a drive to see what others are doing with their yards.

Albany's roots are as old and resonant as anything in America. I move copies of William Kennedy's books back to my bedside table. Kennedy's intimate sense of the city's intricate history. I read the novels in chronological order this time, looking deeply at online maps to unlock further secrets in the interplay of streets and terrain, residences and business.

We moved here for Milo's education. We stay for the house we bought, a 19th century brownstone in a district known as the Mansion Neighborhood. Tall ceilings. Chandeliers. Classical moldings. Marble fireplaces we had cleaned and fixed. Fine art. Carpets. A good place to be.

Velvet curtains frame a streetscape that's equal parts 19th century aspiration and 21st century blight. Ruins with opportunities. The Empire State's remains.

I feel closer to my nation's arc here. Caught Hillary, Kasich, Bernie and Trump in a day's worth of 2016 campaign events.

All history now.

Neighbors barbecue on the street at night, lockdown be damned. They dance on stoops. Weed scent fills the air.

It feels rich. Lawless.

A couple hundred scream outside the Governor's Mansion. MAGA hats. Anti-vaccination signs. Threats against Asians.

I walk up wearing a mask, leashed dog at my side.

When Tiananmen Square happened, I was traveling through our country showing a Renoir film in celebration of the French Revolution's bicentennial. I showed *La Marseillaise* outside. Presented lectures from leading historians before each screening.

My own introductory remarks focused on revolutionary ideas that once rocked each state, and the ways in which the Cold War reinforced our national need for security, safety.

What can I say? I was trying to impress a French woman who wanted to see America. Those were my yearning days. She flew away in Omaha and we never saw each other again.

Another lifetime ago.

"The nobles taught us bad habits. They made us cruel in their image," says Aunaud, the most philosophic of the Provencal peasants at the center of that film I saw seventy plus times. "They're reaping. Reaping what they sowed."

Within two years, the Soviet bloc fell. But so did the Balkans.

I played "The Internationale" instead of "La Marseillaise" before one showing.

No one noticed.

A boarding school memory: Roommates locked in the infirmary. German measles. Figured I'd have our cramped dorm room to myself. Then I got itchy, joined them.

Another pair of memories:

Dad's sadistic game. He'd make my sister shut her eyes. When she opened them my brother and I were instructed not to see her. Played until she broke into tears. Now she says this is her key subject in therapy.

My mother put a nephew into a corner. Everyone visiting her compound on the Eastern Shore of Virginia. Floating candles in the pool. The sound of water fowl rising from the surrounding estuary as fish jumped. We'd put Sam to bed so we could celebrate his mother's birthday.

"I hate this. I hate you," he yelled from a chair where his grandmother had sequestered him.

We left cats behind in England due to quarantine laws. Several times.

Got used to life "outside" in Alaska after college, where the TV broadcast programs a week after they played in the Lower 48.

Had to move my cats when I rented my cabin that summer I traveled with the French woman and Renoir. Renters were allergic. I drove the cats in circles for ten minutes then deposited them and their litter boxes with friends two doors away. They never figured it out.

I'm on the stoop, gauging the street. I read notices from acquaintances intent on outing those not following Covid protocols. They make me uncomfortable. I prefer mixed messages.

Is tribalism creeping into all corners of our lives? Is blame a natural need?

Someone's started setting off fireworks on our street. There's a growing level of crazy, evident in people's cries at night. The fights we hear. The sirens.

I call a cat to my lap. The dog whines. Someone walks pitbulls in our direction.

Should I move the family out of country? Mexico?

We went south of the border when Milo was four. He spent days singing plaintive ranchero laments.

We went into a dark country church where he saw a carved wooden Jesus, painted in blood.

"What did *he* do?" my son asked.

Something was brewing.

Zoom meetings make me grumpy.

I'm competitive. The kids racing up the street in a pack, their mom in pursuit? I'd win. I'd be a better parent.

Gusty. Doors slam. A man yells out.

"It's gonna be coming back with the fall leaves, hit harder 'round Halloween."

He stops before going toward the shelter just up the street.

"Why'd them Chinese make this? They already got us buying all their stuff at the Dollar Store."

"It's a hurting world," I reply.

Some read themselves to sleep. I hug the pillows tighter. My wife heads for the guest room.

The dishwasher is poorly organized. Someone's in the attic. Cat in the freezer? The colander's attached to the kitchen ceiling.

I drift through worries and dreams, cats in my bed.

The dog is with my wife, unbothered by the light she reads by.

Vomit. Starky's right eye is red. Something gray in the black and white cat's other eye.

"Watch the feline sneezes." Right, vet.

Stared myself down in the mirror. Touched my face knowing I've been asked not to. Glared at the pills in my hand.

Aging in a pandemic.

"Your cat, and your dog, has a second eyelid under the first," the vet explains. A masked assistant takes Starky. The dog cries.

"Why does everybody insist on doing one's best all the time when it never really matters how well you do?" asks our son.

Damn *my* eyes. Should I strive for understanding or render what I observe, including the confusion of all striving?

We picked up Milo on his second day. We'd been through a dozen failed adoption attempts and held a Shinto ceremony by a half-frozen waterfall near our house. Burned disposable diapers, chanted, put out a rancid fire with baby formula.

Got the call the next day. Went by the office to sign papers, then headed out to pick up our son.

We went out for dinner and a movie on our last single night together. *The Squid and the Whale*. Reminded us both of my dad, our childhoods in broken homes.

Newborn boy on a couch, swaddled in a onesie and quilted blanket. Peruvian cap on his bald head. Incan flute music on the Long Island home's stereo. A waterway with gulls visible out the ice-framed picture window.

One and a half years earlier we'd brought a girl home from the hospital. Had to return her after 45 days when the birth mother's mother objected to the adoption and decided to accept a mixed-race baby into her extended family. That was the law.

We got Milo home and quarantined ourselves as members of our extended families came like magi. We asked them to stay in hotels. Some never forgave us.

"My family's always stayed together, no matter the size of the house," Fawn explained.

"Same with ours," I answered. "But not now."

Forbearance. A word that invokes patience, restraint, tolerance. Now most know it as a banking term tied to foreclosures and need for some humaneness.

Primary elections are being pushed off. Tax day, too. The president is threatening people. Talking about closing down parts of the postal service.

Forbearance as a means of caring. Of moving us back to ways in which mortality and bereavement, our need for refuge, can be part of our lives once again.

We need new forms of heroism and humility.

Bereavement, refuge, forbearance: A waltz. From the German word for rolling, revolving. Triple time in a close position. Once forbidden, now old-style.

I grab my wife at the bottom of the stairs and dance her through four turns. We hug tight.

I think back to how I lived in imaginary worlds as a boy. Little people and make-believe places. Fairy houses made from twigs and moss, built against rocks and tree roots. Complex drawings of the Children's Crusades. The Black Death. St. Sebastian with his coat of arrows and blood.

Catch myself in the rear-view. I'm alone, no kids in back. It's a new habit.

I pull out boxes that I've stashed away in my office. Weird mementos: snapshots and scribbled notes. Matchbooks. Broken toys. Old drawings and toys from our son's early years.

My mother collected snapshots, placed into albums with black corner fasteners. She sentimentalized the perfect family.

My father saved every letter I'd written him, and carbon copies of all he'd written to me. It wasn't pretty. He'd done the same with everyone he knew. Used the correspondence as evidence when he left my half-sisters' letters that disinherited them.

Dad's was a generation of literary-minded hard drinkers. Every thought, all experience, was heroic and possibly a book. Like those he taught.

I won't open his boxes again. My father's mocking tone lives within me: I never apply myself. I think things are owed to me. My attempts to impress him are feeble. Don't I know what a failure I am?

I described lives he showed no interest in. He dismissed me as sentimental, self-serving. "Just like your naive mother."

I'm ready, at last, to toss it all.

I keep the radio on. It's like therapy: a chorus of community voices. I'm helping to run a station, making sure the pieces fit. Listening for mishaps. Ensuring we get the word out on Covid.

"Corona don't attack your butt," one producer says in a public service announcement. "No need to hoard."

I'd started out playing pieces from the state's health commissioner, but he sounded defensive. Tried the governor, Cuomo, but he felt mean. Settled on the World Health Organization's clips, then decided we needed our own voices.

We repeat the butt-attack PSA a lot. Add others' voices. Soften our music.

Things grow tougher. We start up a daily calendar of food pick-up sites, testing clinics, tips for avoiding eviction.

Are we ready for the long haul?

A memory rises: I was living in the eighteen-room house next to a cemetery in West Kill, New York. Gave a writing exercise to my elementary-school journalism class.

"Describe someone in this room so we can guess who it is," I instructed.

Two-thirds wrote about an overweight, aging guy pretending he wasn't going bald. He'd ponytailed what hair he still had and grown a Van Dyke.

Then this recurring fear. I've grown my hair long, swept it back into a ponytail. Let it reach my shoulders. Then it tangles. Tangles even more into gnarly knots.

I cut it all off.

Several months into quarantine and I am ready for a barber.

"Whatever happens, Dad, don't get a mullet," says my son.

A mutton-chopped dude in a face mask shaves Milo's sides, leaves the top long.

I get another old man's cut in the old-style tile-walled and dark wood barbershop filled with photos going back into the Depression years and earlier. This city was a destination, then, a place I'd like to have visited. The muse of Bill Kennedy's cycle of novels.

Covid's got me searching.

Something chews above me. I check to see if a cat's stuck. The sound is louder in the guest bedroom. Nothing amiss.

A skunk once lived under our previous home's living room. Sprayed each time heavy bass lines played on my stereo.

Had a timing belt go in Manhattan. Came back to a wide-eyed mechanic babbling about tooth marks all over the undercarriage of my Datsun.

"I found mouse turds," my wife says coming down from the attic. "We need more traps."

I zoom my dermatologist. Put my largest shirt on backwards, sit on the edge of a table looking at my phone's Covid feed, wondering if there is an app I'd be able to scan my skin with.

"Please wait," the nurse says. "The doctor will be with you shortly."

I scolded my dad for trying to make his doctors like him.

"Don't joke," I'd say. "Use your time to impart and glean information."

I ask my doctor if I should strip. She laughs.

My father would have loved this sort of doctoring. He was convinced of his charm.

> **The Japanese term** *kuchisabishii* translates as "longing to have or put something in one's mouth."
>> *Wabi-sabi* captures the idea of the perfectly imperfect.
>> Their combination defines my Covid life. A new zeitgeist?

I speak with friends, local and faraway, about restaurants. Might be better for our weight than endless trips to the kitchen.

I used to love places where I got the sense that there may be no better place.

Now, we agree, we'd take anything. Diners, pizza parlors, theme restaurants.

We want entertainment as much as food.

> **I have to write obituaries about people I knew.** I've been at the newspaper for over three decades.

Lynda Marie, 59, was "blessed with the bluest of eyes, a beautiful smile and a spirited personality; as well as the ability to take on all challenges. She had previously lost her husband, and will be missed by aunts, uncles, nieces and nephews."

> Dominic, 85, worked as a toll collector on the Rip Van Winkle Bridge, loved playing cards, going to the casino, doing scratch-offs, watching television. "He was an avid bowler and golfer and enjoyed camping and hunting back in the day." He loved everyone he met and had a way of expressing his joy "with his hands."

> **Big dreams? Gotta try, right?**
> I met a young man from Tonawanda who worked behind the counter at the Catskill McDonald's. He talked

about having run with a crystal meth crowd after his mom split town. She didn't tell him where or why she was going.

The dude was spending time in our renter's apartment. Less macho than the usual type. He got along well with Milo, too. He had vulnerability wrapped in a boxer's physique.

Mike had dreams, too. He was training at Cus D'Amato's gym above the police station, trying to straighten his life out the way Mike Tyson had. We talked for hours about the things his mom had told him about his dad. About the ladies he liked. How he knew it wasn't his time for love. He had to get his game back first.

Then he disappeared.

I worked with a guru who failed to find a following. Watched friends sour after their marriages floundered. Wrote about political dreamers who lose more than they win.

I know how it is to give up. How hard it is to shoot the moon and fail.

I met my wife when she was married to an older man. There was mystery to her: pure white hair bobbed atop a lithe young body. Met her when she was wearing a ski suit. Ageless.

She divorced. I interviewed her for an hour, wrote a feature profile about her work as an artist and community activist. Decided I'd had enough yearning, chasing those I should have pegged as unavailable. Friendship with Fawn was enough.

We started dance classes. I proposed a week after our first night together. We married within the year. Started therapy before we fought, the better to prepare for a long haul.

"Shall we adopt," I asked after months of hormone injections and aided insemination.

"I'm ready now," Fawn replied as we sat on the stone steps to my godfather Paul's house in the High Peaks district of the Adirondacks, bears keening in the darkening distance.

Fawn and I married twice. Once as an elopement, the second time a more public event a half year later. We still celebrate those and two other anniversaries on a quarterly basis.

Took me years to get past a fear that she would move on. I was sure I'd fuck things up. Even after we adopted Milo and found ourselves stable, I'd measure the time we were together against her previous relationships.

Had I inherited my anxiety? Is it really gone now?

"I think this has been good for us," she says as we lie in bed listening to our street's noises. I turn on the baby monitor. Gentle waves.

"It's been easier with you," I reply.

The cleaning lady comes for the first time in months. A sign of normalcy, of reopening.

The afternoon sun spins brightness and shadow across the former high school's brick wall that overlooks our back garden. I have a book of Winslow Homer seascapes beside me. Ben Webster's big sax, screeching kids, and distant rap serves as a soundtrack.

Triggered memories: Late afternoons in Manhattan. The front porch at my Echo Notch home. Same music playing, on a hifi instead of my phone. Lilac giving way to the rise of fireflies, the descent of August stars.

Sitka. Putney Mountain in southeast Vermont and the hills around Gambier, Ohio. The South Devon Coast. Catskills when the mist rises like chimney smoke over dead-end cloves.

A myriad. Landscapes collaged.

"Look at this," my wife says, passing her phone to me.

"So?"

"Look at the different ways light plays on the building."

What makes certain moments epiphanies? What prepares the mind to reach beyond?

"It's done through an algorithm," Fawn adds.

I prefer to think of it as magic, captured.

We drive seventy-five miles up the Northway for Thai food. Want to go to where our son first tried Pad Thai.

"I know it's a long way, but nothing we've tried since has been as good," Milo says.

I think of his grandfather. Nothing was as good, for dad, as his memories. His experience.

"I can't wait for them to put the hoops back up," Milo says from the back seat, dog's head in his lap.

"More time outside," Fawn chides. "Less time on your phone and Playstation."

The dog sits up; looks longingly at the passing forest.

I'm not sure what I want anymore. I've started to enjoy lockdown; I take a smug satisfaction in our split nation. I'm hoping to find a passage beyond memory.

The car is sliding. I think I'm alone. Was there something or someone in the passenger's seat? A presence? A shadow? An echo? Then comes a noiseless crunch.

I recognize the dream, lift myself out of the ghost-world. Wake.

A brackish lake in the Adirondack foothills. Miles of pine. A couple warns me and my son, then four, about leeches. We wade in anyway. As I wipe dark wigglers off our legs a half hour later I swear him to secrecy.

"Wheeches," Milo yelled, jubilant. He ran to Fawn and her friends around the dining table. "I got wheeches, Mommy! Wheeches."

> ***Normal People, Outlander. Run. Watchmen.*** Streaming as a substitute for couple's therapy? A national reckoning?
> Can we agree to do better?
> Catharsis isn't catharsis once it slips into endlessly repeating stasis.

The marriage crashes down around us. We threaten to or actually hit each other. Maybe it would help relieve some of the sludge-like pressure we both feel. How can we get well? What's the fix?

These are the roles we play, at home, in friendships. The worst of times.

> **My mother led** reconstructive therapy sessions for families and insisted on taking her various husbands to week-long therapy training sessions once a year.
> Dad specialized in sensitivity training with students at the women's colleges where he taught. The hip teacher with a beard and motorcycle. Later, he dated one of his shrinks. Married one of his students.

> > **My wife and I** returned to therapy regularly. The first time came when Fawn felt I needed to handle work pressures

48 better. Then we wanted to bolster communication as we
approached parenthood.

My dad asked if I could father a new kid for him and
his wife. Just a simple sperm donation. That didn't sit well
as we struggled to adopt.

More for our therapist.

Fawn's work grew intense, She had to escape the ten-
sions our obstinate boy caused, the pressure of my bot-
tomless needs. Things snapped and we stopped sleeping
together for most of a year. We took individual therapists,
plus joint counseling each week.

We found a shrink for Milo, and sometimes all went to
Doctor Doug as a family.

We clambered to a better place. Acknowledged fault
lines. Somehow got better.

We're glad to be driving less. One less worry. Too many
years watching for that odd patch of black ice, those slippery winter hills. A drunk driver or someone texting.

Health, we keep learning, is work.

Music summons the kid in me, in all of us. Mr. Ding-a-Ling, the neighborhood's ice cream man, is out and about. A sign of reprieve? Forbearance?

I dream of driving, safely, to a riverside mansion that looks out across water to distant mountains. I'm ready for vivid sunsets, for a symphony.

Loose change for a rainbow pop, a hand-held sundae.

Have to hold on to what childhood's left.

Our eldest cat CP (for Cutie Pie) has a pair of duplicate stuffed bears. We collectively call them Baby. She took to the bears soon after we got her, when she was smaller than my palm. Lynn, who found CP, said the kitten's mother and the rest of the litter had been killed by coyotes.

I stayed home with CP her first month. She'd suckle my pinkie.

Our son kept stuffed animals. The dog chewed out their eyes and un-stuffed them. We found CP after she found her Baby and pulled it from the dog's pile. She had nested beneath this white plush animal twice her size, eyes rolled into her head as she suckled happily. We bought her a second Baby soon after.

If only we could each have a Baby like CP's.

The weather heats up, and Covid numbers rise. Masks come off. The street's louder than ever.

Our President is always angry.

We are all looking for curves to flatten.

I count blessings: communal gardens; street fridges filled with free food; a shift, in our street's soundtrack, from hard rap to Quiet Storm, Motown.

The lights on the Corning Tower, our city's tallest structure, have been arranged to spell "NY Tough." It was meant for our frontline workers, those dealing with disease. Albany takes it as a nod to our ongoing battle to not only survive but maybe even thrive once more.

Shootings around the neighborhood. Stabbings in the parks.

Milo hooks up with some friends who have been at home too. I drive them out to where I've seen basketball hoops on a college campus.

"Whatever happened to all those kids you knew at the library," Albizu asks as we drive through West Hill, center to much of the city's strife.

I see a group of kids outside a cordoned-off play-ground. We pull up and stop. I roll down my window as my son and his friends cringe.

"Mister Paul! Mister Paul!" they yell, running up to the car unmasked.

I fist-bump the two youngest at the front of the pack, the rest holding back with wary eyes.

Do they know I'm a swagman, my life but a waltz?

We picked the free school our son attends to help assuage his tics, build his social skills, get him street-savvy. He learned to look people in the eye.

I'm a writer; I can justify anything. I gave up "because-I-told-you-so" parenting long ago.

Zoomed education? It never had a chance.

I've tried to push my kid to recognize heart, the emotion driving art. Science. Politics. The ways our culture can hide responses to the challenges we face over and over.

I start the complex application process for visas, health insurance and a place to live and get educated for what would be his sophomore year in high school. In Mexico.

"What do you think a civil war will look like?"

Milo and his friends are talking. Our neighborhood is black-majority, with few businesses. The folks at the liquor store down the street stay open. Jerry's corner deli, holding down the corner for forty-plus years, mumbles about closing shop.

"They may own the skies but we rats down here know our alleys."

Black man in a gas mask. Milo and I in the street, facing police in riot gear, our shirts soaked in milk. Best way to clean out tear gas.

We watch a city councilmember pushed away by angry police.

"I don't care if you live down there," says the cop. "Blame the protesters."

Fawn and I wait on the stoop for Milo,
out with his friends.

Gas mask man walks by again. Lifts
his face covering.

"And so it starts," he says.

We speak in code; George Floyd days. It
feels like a reckoning.

Taking the dog for a walk in a hemlock forest. We hear
gunfire in the distance; the rapid-fire of target practice.
What are shooters practicing for?

What gets looted? Box stores, banks, check-cashing and cell-phone
shops. Government buildings.

An angry man tells the chief of police: "You gotta teach your troops
to understand and respect black rage. You can't treat the man who's
yelling as a threat. He can't help it."

After months of Covid, it's becoming difficult not to
complain. Fawn and I speak of our dead parents.

"Your mom would have hated all this," she says.
"But she would have fought with Jim, taking the side
of masks and other precautions."

I too had fought her final husband, a former nuclear scientist who
became an avid Fox fan. He challenged the will his wife, my mother,
wrote before he entered her life.

We knew where our siblings' spouses stood, afraid or angry, about
pandemic precautions and the George Floyd protests. My sister's husband was confrontational, always backing the power. Fawn's brother-

in-law was a Trump fan, recently retired into a world of
oldies television and online Facebook rants.

Her dad, in Florida, was taking all precautions.

My dad? He had abdicated, sick of all that preceded
this, long, long ago.

Our son and his friends were learning
history as it happened.

The library director chokes up on the
weekly zoom meeting, reading a letter
he'd written about small businesses that
have been looted. His dad had owned a
small business.

Libraries have been closed for months. Then they
boarded up against the threat of looting.

Too bad we're trained to side with business rather
than people. And communities.

Libraries may be the last truly democratic institution. People apply for jobs, pay bills there. They notarize the documents our society
demands of those living on the edge.

Librarians train to deal with a public in crisis, people caught in trauma.

But they're also taught to always act as professionals. To chill the warmth of the places they work in.

F awn and I drive to a monastery. We need an escape.

I spent years with Maronites in Massachusetts on a monthly basis. It was a form of writer's retreat. I followed the monks' schedule of masses and meals in exchange for a room and writing porch. Chants and a daily mass, starting at 5:30. Silence. Lights out before 10.

I was there the weekend after 9/11. I left when John Paul II died.

I'm not a religious person, but I love ritual. I respect those who feel spirit moving in them.

One time at Holy Trinity I came across a moose in the woods. We both stared at each other, then darted.

I saw a monk and started to tell him. He raised a finger to his lips. I nodded, put splayed fingers by my head, thumbs to my ears. He smiled and nodded.

Leaving a few days later, the monastery's abbot waved me over.

"I heard you saw our moose," he said. "Are you ready for baptism?"

"I *am* slipping from atheism to agnosticism," I replied.

That was our joke.

I moved nineteen times by the time I finished college. Added on another sixteen homes since. I bring this up with pride but also consternation. I wish I knew a place fully, decade after decade; felt a town or city deep in my bones. Do I lack empathy?

Guilty? I guess. Privileged? In so many ways.

These are the questions of the day.

I stretch my imagination as best I can.

My co-worker Rita's reaction to the recent protests—to this long season of disease, economic collapse, and a vengeful leader's nasty provocations—is based on something her grandfather told her on his deathbed. Read the Book of Revelations. Read it backwards.

Revelation means unveiling, from *revelare:* to lay bare. Seven seals. False gods. Boiling seas of blood, plague, mass destruction. A thousand-year pause before it all happens again, worse.

It does read better backwards. Start at the end and the bad gets washed away.

Rita claims forty-three siblings begat by her gospel-singer father. Better, in her eyes, to deal with the unknowable by concentrating on the willed-for.

I sit up for our son. My wife's request. He and his fellow teen justice warriors are marching around the city.

Young kids in the street, their moms on one stoop, dads and uncles on the next. Food on grills; a table brought out with salads. A birthday cake with nine candles. It's past midnight and muggy.

Lockdown is officially lifting. Dancing is in order.

"They offered me cake but I asked for a smoked turkey leg," says Milo, coming in. "I'm happy we're here."

A flash of white. A bird lands on electric wires, face mask dangled from its beak.

More protests. Remove the statuary that advertises white supremacy!

Removal's stages of grief: remorse, anger, shame, anxiety, insouciance.

I grew up in Virginia, learned about the War of Northern Aggression. Studied the English Civil War at a Church of England school. Traveled through Europe twenty years after World War II, fascinated by the French Revolution and Napoleon. Visited Dachau the year it became a museum. I was eight.

Pain eventually paralyzes. Or it becomes a memory we can hold in our hands.

We use what we can to build new nests.

How to appreciate our mortality? I knew a ghost. I never saw her, but I learned to describe her for those that asked if my house was haunted.

She wore a black dress, buttoned high at the collar. Her hair was up, wound into a tight bun with streaks of gray. Laced high-top boots with a middling heel. A corset that pinched.

There was no anger in my home's ghost. Bereavement and grief, accompanied by forbearance, in her hazel eyes.

A man showed up who'd grown up in that house.

"You ever see a sad-eyed woman here?" he had asked. "I never saw her but could tell you what she looked like."

Three months of New York on Pause and I am itching to spend money. I want to go shopping in claustrophobic book and record shops. I want to ride the wooden escalators of classic high-ceilinged department stores redolent of Chanel.

New York City friends tell me the avenues are empty, everything closed. A barrage of sirens. Same in Berkeley, Seattle, L.A.

We try to sort out what has slipped, what is holding. What should, could or would change.

"You'll need an official Covid-19 test result, negative. Plus proof of a two-week quarantine at home," says the hotel rep. "It's law, not policy."

The hotels I call in Vermont say that New Yorkers should stay home.

We get a cabin by a restaurant on Lake Ontario, far from anyone, that started as a bootlegger's getaway. They knew about lockdown.

I drift back to past travels and try sorting them.

Before my marriage, I traveled with mother. Drove to the hot springs of Circle, Alaska in January. Journeyed down coast roads from Maine to Sarasota. Found her a new home where she eventually found that last husband, Jim.

Picked my father up, once, fresh from a detox month at Hazelden. Drove from the Cleveland airport into Canada at Niagara Falls. Ferried from Charlevoix, Quebec, to the Gaspe Peninsula, which we rounded as he slept. Watched the Tidal Bore at Moncton, New Brunswick.

Not so much vacations, or adventures, as passages that made their passings bearable.

I wished I could have spoken with them about death, then and later. I still don't know whether the failure was mine or theirs.

We flew to Missouri as a family when Obama/Biden faced John McCain and Sarah Palin. Picked up Fawn's mom and drove her to a family reunion in Christian County, Kentucky.

Working tobacco farms and old log cabins. I meandered my way, kid napping in the back, to the Jefferson Davis Memorial State Park. It was home to our republic's fifth tallest monument, a lonely 351-foot obelisk to a fallen man memorialized six decades after his ignoble defeat.

How do you take down such a bad idea?

"Everyone used to play music together, tell stories from the old days," my wife said. "They used to make their own pies and salads, smoked hams and fried chicken."

Instead of people exchanging remembered songs, televisions ran constantly, even on the porches.

Did such people ever dance? Fawn can't remember. I think of my grandmothers laughing as they tried to Charleston. Solo dancing.

I let a wordless waltz rise to a murmured tune. At least some of us can still move with meaning.

A rambling thought: I've had surrogate children. I've had surrogate parents. I am starting to feel like I might need a surrogate country. Protests, rallies, legal action; shifting presidential polls raise my hopes.

We're trained to look for better. I went away to school early, my choice, and envied those from other backgrounds. I substituted theirs for mine.

I watch my son play basketball in our backyard. The court is brick, the hoop too small.

Two of the pairs of brothers have divorced parents. Two other boys are plagued by anxiety.

I don't see any of them looking for surrogacy. Or dancing. Yet.

We learn about being ignored before we can roll over. It's a toughen-up tactic.

Silence builds. A teacher claims not to see your raised hand. Job applications get no response. Unanswered emails, calls. Your questions are stupid. You're not good enough. You've failed.

We learn to cry louder. We cry ourselves to sleep.

We reach beyond ourselves. We learn courage.

My wife asks why I can't hear her. My kid repeats a question over and over. Our city explodes with anger.

We do our best. We can always try to do better.

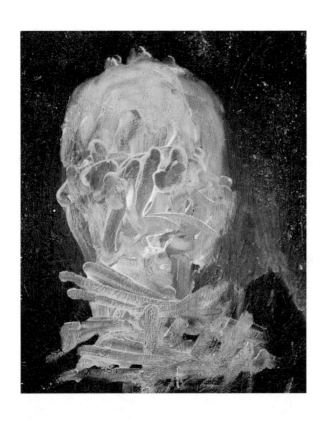

A **couple married.** He left the bachelor's pad he'd retreated to after his last marriage. She rented out the home where she had raised her kids. They honeymooned in the Caribbean, made a new home in a Brooklyn high-rise.

Covid hit. The husband did his Wall Street work from the guest bedroom. The wife tutored on-line from the kitchen. George Floyd's murder. The couple watched marchers gather on the plaza far below. They sniped at each other.

He said things he didn't know how to take back. They stopped talking.

So many friends dead. Rick, Chester, Gus, McDonough. Liz, my girlfriend of a dozen years post-college. Some expected; some still mysterious. All pre-pandemic. We each build our own internal monuments to those lost, including our own lost aspirations.

Everyone in the car looking at phones.
Memories from my single days:

Deep country, upstate New York. Editing a local paper, circulation a few thousand. Town board meetings. Party lines. A zoning-board member shows up in pajamas. An entire room of elected officials falls asleep in a town clerk's overheated kitchen.

People yell at each other, then linger near their cars, laughing in the chilly air as it starts to snow.

Spirit. How lucky we'd be if that could remain. Without meanness, mind you.

Milo, at two, asleep on my bare chest. "Infant thug," says Uncle M after the kid had a screaming fit and punched at me. At eight, he brought a ring at Walmart for one of the twins (they were six); had to chase her around the school to give it to her. Sleepover fears at ten:

"Please get me. Now."

"It's 200 miles."

"Pleeaase Daddy?"

Pets and friends and now these months at home, gaming online. Fawn and I see the man emerging from our boy.

I knew I had to out my brother's heroin habit when he came to my home with the flu, bad. Soiled himself in the car. Spent his time in bed. It was only a couple of months since he got married in my living room. He admitted his addiction. Cried.

I said he'd have to tell his wife before they headed for Mexico. You can't spring cold turkey on her.

"It's why I'm here," he said. "I don't want to tell her."

When he confessed she threw him out. Canceled the honeymoon. I later drove to the Lower East Side, asked around at shooting galleries until I found him.

A few years later, David seemed to find peace in a Harlem apartment. He rejoined NA, was seeing a shrink. We made plans for Christmas Eve at St. John the Divine Cathedral.

Wild-eyed David at the door of his walk-up. A chaos of ripped-open upholstery, broken chairs and plates. Scattered clothes.

"It's bugs, man," he said, showing me scraped and bleeding arms. "They're everywhere. I brought them back from Mexico."

He pulled his last remaining bowl from a cupboard.

"See, they're everywhere."

I saw nothing.

He broke the bowl and broke into tears.

David died of a speedball in an SRO hotel. The D.C. cops found lipstick traces on a cigarette butt in a cup-turned-ashtray. No one followed up. We couldn't.

I miss my brother. We gave Milo his middle name. They never met.

I hope this story resonates enough to keep my boy safer than my brother ever was. Troubles cascade. They go away. But they return, and they keep coming.

I **want to see friends.** Want to know whether our eyes, our mouths, look different. Would we rush to hug only to pause and then step back, blushing like teenagers?

In our sixties, we see age lines, time passed. We want to step back into earlier selves, losing our scars and fat.

Competing marches. A couple hundred white anti-vaxxers in front of the governor's mansion. Kids and parents—one-third white, one-third Black, one-third Latino—head for Lincoln Park.

They chant: "Black Little League Matters."

No fights. No taunts. Just fear again.

Milo's Free School graduation: We had to throw a party.

Eleven boys from the neighborhood who've spent the last month together, pulled from home by the protests. By basketball in our back yard.

The pandemic pushes me past coolness. I cherish my years of yearning but spent enough time steeling myself to rejection.

I am tired of rampant cynicism. I welcome the sentimental. Whatever is heartfelt.

Daily aches and pains. This fact of aging. Raging illness all around.
My friends feel it too.

Fireworks are louder. We learn to separate the hollow pops of gunfire from M-80s and the bigger booms that echo the cops' use of stun bombs.
Inching towards Independence Day.

Sixteen people shot in one week, two fatalities.
"Dudes are getting guns younger. Middle schoolers," says Jerome. "Same dudes handing out fireworks from their trunks. Ghost stuff."
Jerome's with SNUG, ex-gang members who've spent time in prison. They're intent on breaking the cycle of violence and incarceration.
"Corona broke things," he says. "People are letting off steam. They're getting riled up by social media. Disses and no one remembers how to step back anymore."

I get an email from Donald J. Trump. He selected me for his Trump 100 Club, which includes a possible all-expenses-paid trip to some place where I'd have my photo taken with him, one of one hundred Patriots (capital P) honored.
I didn't make my contribution by 11:59 p.m.
"Is everything okay?" came the next missive. "President Trump asked if you were available to meet him at an upcoming event, but we told him we hadn't heard from you yet. The President is going to call us again soon for an update. Can we confirm your RSVP when he calls?"
No.

A friend calls in tears. She'd spent decades building her career. Gave up her marriage. Covid hit.

"I've been a half-year without work. My savings are gone," she says. "I'm going to have to move out of the City."

I know how hard this is for her. I want my friend to keep the faith, to know there's still love and support here for all of us.

I have good work. A savings account. A portfolio my money man says will work out fine.

"Just don't look at it," he adds.

I look anyway. Slippage has been going on now for months. It seems forever.

Would we make it to the end? Would we all end up swagmen, waltzing our Matildas coast to coast? Or worse, facing undreamed-of shores?

I go back into the library every other week, masked, gloved, socially distanced. My wife went back to her office weeks ago. Our dog and cats are needier than usual.

"Look, we're here. Been here all day. Where were you?" they seem to ask, loudly and insistently. "We thought you were dead!"

I already miss my all-home routine, similar to my life before I needed jobs that would cover our family's health insurance. I'd been all freelance for far too long.

Now comes the hard work: Figuring out how I want my life to progress. Convincing my son that there are still good things ahead. That one still needs to work to make life meaningful.

He's not convinced. Well, neither am I. I'm still learning.

"**My kid slipped a cog.** He punched me again."
A co-worker is talking about what a pleasure his son was through high school. Then came divorce. Father and son quarantined together and something snapped. The young man stopped taking his meds, stole his dad's laptop and phone. Broke his ankle but refused help. Chose to be homeless.

The son of my wife's boss heard voices. He cut himself. An intervention was needed but no appointments were possible. Too dangerous, given the pandemic.

Personal finances have always determined what cars we drive, how we school our kids, when and where we eat out, where we live. They shape our fears, our politics, our future.

Now it's affecting our health, our ability to feel for others, to empathize.

This is no longer a complaint but a challenge. Can one will a renaissance?

Remember the early-1970s Comprehensive Employment and Training Act that promised to build a new public works program as the Vietnam War and its protests started to fade from public consciousness?

Signed into law by Nixon, grown during the Carter era, then transformed beyond recognition under Reagan, CETA allowed the growth of arts organizations and environmental efforts, and found work for young people unsure of what to do with their liberal arts degrees.

My mother moved to Alaska for a new marriage and work at a fine arts camp. My dad hired the help he needed to revive a struggling arts colony. I worked with the U.S. Forest Service, replanting clearcut Alaskan forest, writing and editing environmental planning documents, running a newsletter.

CETA made it possible to start community radio stations.

I get a different song caught in my craw. An American version of Banjo's waltz. "The Big Rock Candy Mountain," precursor to a pile of American hobo tunes.

I'm goin' to stay
Where you sleep all day
Where they hung the jerk
That invented work.
In the big Rock Candy Mountain.

Took Fawn and the dog to a drive-in. The start of her birthday week. Cooked lamb chops, polenta, a spinach salad.

People wore masks when entering the biergarten. Everyone socially distanced. Lawn chairs; mosquitoes. A man in a hoodie tried out card tricks.

"Isn't it nice to be out," came the announcer's voice.

We clapped at the show's finale, as much for the sliver moon and endless stars as for being with a crowd of like-minded cinephiles. I had the sense that we will persevere, somehow.

Six hollow pops in a row, a long pause, then a half dozen more. Sirens. Early afternoon. A man shot twice in the back, running, then shot point blank, repeatedly, as he lay on the sidewalk.

A few days later a seventeen-year-old is arrested. Got tied to three more shootings, including a three-year-old who got a bullet through the arm as he napped in daycare.

They say the young man was lost to the streets. I remember him from the library.

I double down on my choice to read fiction. To write more. To think more deeply.

I focus again on our plans to leave, to find a new refuge in Mexico.

The first piece I ever published, "Sanded Men," was about learning insomnia from my father. About listening to him justify his tumble into divorce from my mother.

Mom hated people staying up late. She also disliked those who woke early, thinking something was wrong.

Dad would sit up all hours, drinking and scribbling in notebooks. Letters. Complaints.

I go to bed early now. Write best in the morning.

I've given up trying to wake my son.

I hang in the kitchen with Milo and his buddies. The gang is headed to the Empire State Plaza, a few blocks up the hill from our home, where they're on a first-name basis with the state police who protect New York's capitol.

"We like the way the city looks at night," Silas says.

"Everything has its time," adds Milo. "We're still kids now."

Our garden's new Hostas and Rose of Sharon bloom.

I promise my wife this will be our last summer without

central AC, although we'll keep the window unit in our bedroom to cut down on street noise.

More memories, pre-pandemic, rise with the noise of mid-summer. I turn them into blogs, trying to push past memoir into a glimpse of the ways Covid has crept into all our heads. Reaching beyond complaint to build stronger understanding.

> **My father** in the cemetery house's kitchen, talking about visiting the Soviet Union at its end. Massive printings of literature, the fact that there were no phone books.
>
> I've kept some of my phone books ever since, yellow pages included.
>
> We build our own world of contacts now. We live on little islands.

I spent one Fourth of July watching Wimbledon while a muscled dude did pull-ups on the television rack attached to the Sullivan County jail's concrete walls. I'd been caught driving with a suspended license.

I'd gotten shoplifting charges as a younger man, one in England, the other at the beach when my grandmother was chaperoning. I spent a night in lockup for public drunkenness.

I share these things with my son. He's been telling us his friends smoke pot.

> **I practice a delicate dance:** acknowledging the wrongheadedness of past actions while avoiding braggadocio. Guess I also wanted to raise his estimation of me beyond just a dad.

"Mistakes are human," I tell my son. "Some people make few, others live with abandon. You've got to admit the fuckups then move on to better."

"Like you have," he answers.

Being an older dad once took the bite out of aging. Then my parents died. We started getting two and sometimes three AARP magazines a month.

Precancerous growths on my scalp and arm. My dermatologist shoots nitrogen into my flesh, and it hurts like hell.

Sure, my son's friends think I'm cool. But that hasn't put a stop to how heavy I feel each evening as I climb my stairs to bed. Or my fears of inheriting my parents' foibles or falling prey to incessant complaining.

Going back: I recall how you entered the Chapman Hotel through a living room. Down the road was a trailer bar in a landfill. Melody Manor's owner and bar mistress wore a polka-dot dress, Wellingtons and a bouffant wig. She sang and sashayed to the 45's on her vintage jukebox: Shirelles, Barbara Lee, Baby Washington. The Ronettes!

Drinking histories tell of a region's roadhouses where you kept a mug behind the bar, the head of a shot deer on the wall. I spent time for a while at a field worker's bar with jerked goat on dance nights. Wrote histories of long-gone bars and their apocryphal legends.

Good old days? How about relics of a pre-DWI world that harkened back to when Dutch Schultz and Legs Diamond escaped their city enterprises to maintain rural underworld empires. A mix of city folk in heartland America. Apple cider distilled to something just short of deadly, but hugely profitable during Prohibition.

Young boys brought Babe Ruth buckets of lukewarm beer as he fished Catskills creeks. The tales linger where nothing else replaces them.

What tales are ready to be told now?

I stopped drinking around my dad, then around my mother. Friends gave up pot. Some pre-Covid. Others frightened by their lockdown selves.

Generations turn. One-two-three. Again.

A fourteen-year-old with pants slung below his ass threatened to shoot *my* ass. A drunk homeless man put a leaking bag on a desk and the entire library smelled of beer. Two sisters got in a fight, broke glasses, tore out the other's carefully braided extensions. Someone spat on a librarian. A brick bounced off our window.

A six-year-old came to check out two volumes of the Library of America's collected William James. He returned them minutes later.

"Ain't no pictures," he said sweetly. "What else you got?"

Two brothers hugged me, stinking of piss. I sat with them out front of the library.

"Why they have to kick us out again? Don't they know we got anger issues?"

I shouldn't have told anyone this: My swimming
hole is five minutes from my old home. We'd go at all hours. Kim kept a bungalow that overlooked the junction of two creeks, a scene he painted repeatedly over the decades.

I swam laps through pockets of cool, cold, and sometimes warm water. Fish fry nibbled my toes. A dog-sized trout eyed the world from darker depths.

We were sworn to secrecy.

Now all I want is for us to go there again, to be together. To share.

My blog sinks to maudlin.
I scrape at old scabs. I revisit old epiphanies.
Keeping hope alive is work. Especially this election year.

The radio is a lifeline. But we want something more than pandemic tips and daily Covid updates.

I find themes to repeat, musical interludes to build on the moment. Sharing vibes.

Started with several versions of "O-o-h Child" by The Five Stairsteps, Nina Simone, Valerie Carter and Laura Nyro. Played a lot of "A Love Supreme" after the riots began. Not time yet for Beethoven adagios, sounds from the Depression. Thank god.

I decide to stop making decisions for others. Let them choose what's right for their listeners' ears. This is community radio; let each producer find their own means of making things lighter. Or not.

A soliloquy from Orson Welles' *The Magnificent Ambersons,* based on Booth Tarkington's novel about change in an earlier America.

The family patriarch struggles to make sense of his daughter's death of a broken heart. He looks into a fire and drifts into his thoughts.

"It must be in the sun! There wasn't anything here but the sun in the first place, and the earth came out of the sun, and we came out of the earth. Whatever we are, we must have been in the sun. We go back to the earth we came out of, so the earth will go back to the sun that it came out of. And time means nothing —nothing at all—so in a little while we'll all be back in the sun together."

My first yearning: Elaine Dameron's dark hair, straight as her family. Loose strands in front of each ear.

She held my hand during services at the Presbyterian Church. Sixth grade and I was ready for God. Or a courtship blessed by holiness.

It never took.

My first cousin once removed was a major force in the Southern Baptist Council. A VIP VP.

"Are you brave enough for baptism," he asked me repeatedly when I stayed with him in my teens.

Years later, I tried the rural congregations close to home.

"Are you shopping for religion?" a pastor asked me. "Take your time."

I was looking for new friends, new experiences. Love of a deeper pedigree.

Few attended. All have closed.

One of us would call the others for dinner. We came from France, Germany, various places down South or out in the Midwest. We had big homes with extra bedrooms. There were long drives, the dodging of suicidal deer.

Dancing after dinner. Nights, seasons, molted into each other. We'd go home with borrowed clothing and books, new ideas.

Then it was gone. Fleche and Puanani, who'd depart each summer for the south of France, moved away. Richard and Laura had a kid. Sue and Steve got swallowed by careers. I found love, got married.

Sitting at a beach restaurant on the Breton coast, our sons playing in the chilly water, Martina recited a poem I wrote for her. I couldn't remember it, but I recognized the feeling.

We took a photo of our boy outside Disney World when he was three months old.

"There," I joked. "We can tell him he's already been."

He learned to crawl in Montreal, went to the Metropolitan Opera on his first birthday, got strings of beads strung around his neck in New Orleans. Milo first walked on a Northern California beach as seals brayed in the background.

Mermaids banged the glass before his sleeping face at Weekee Wachee Springs.

"You're spending on nothing," said Fawn's mother. "He won't remember anything but that he's been spoiled."

I traveled as a kid. My wife didn't.

Fawn didn't like road trips so the many stopovers I researched were for her as much as Milo. And me. Ditto the marathon twenty-playground weekends with a Chinatown rest stop; friends who had heard about our fun came along for the ride.

Eventually Milo said he was eyeing college overseas.

"And I never want to go to Disney," he added.

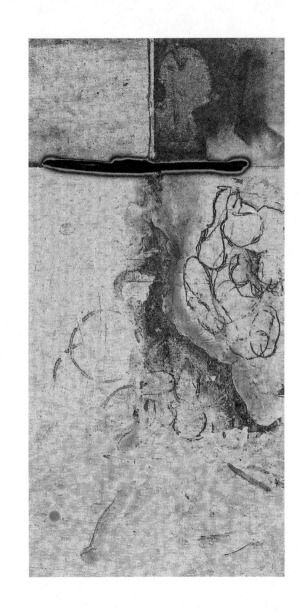

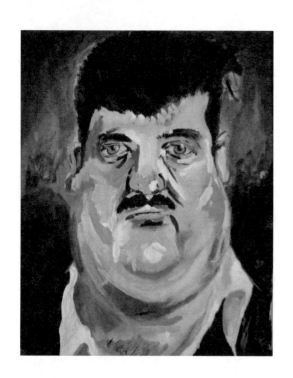

I **list some picayune** white-people worries. At the top: my dislike for the way our cleaning lady rearranges things.

Note the "our." We called them maids when I was growing up down south. Said they were family but never had them over. Visited their homes wide-eyed as if on field trips.

My dad was a mean tickler. We'd beg him to stop. The usual tears. Sometimes pee.

A *New York Times* story pointed out how a laughing face is much like a panicked one. Socrates described tickling as more pain than pleasure.

I ask Milo what he thinks of tickling. He shrugs.

"I *will* play sleeping giant if you want," he answers, naming another of my father's games; we'd climb atop him as he pretended to sleep, to be swallowed by his hairy body, his smoking drinker's scent.

Maybe we are moving forward. Breaking old dance patterns.

The newspapers I worked for have folded. I miss it—the people I worked with, laying out pages, distributing the paper, even fielding requests to publish corrections. I miss the camaraderie, the deadlines, that way of seeing and working with the world.

I once wrote a story in which I listed everyone I wrote for, explaining how I cobbled together a living wage. I charted the way pay affected copy: Dailies paid by the column inch, plus a meetings fee. You pulled as many stories as you could get out of single events. Weekly publications had a higher flat fee that inspired a sense of style, the depths more serious writing demands.

I imagined my readers for each publication.

Lifetimes. Loss. We like to think our work is epic and needed.

I call old editors, fellow writers, and we speak about what's happening. We want to help. But how?

I stopped writing poetry when I found I could no longer read my own whiny words. The voice I'd nurtured had phrasing, observations, and a touch of music. But the overarching sentiment was no longer something I identified with.

I had pegged my future to poetry. Ginsberg said I'd do better riding the MTA than studying towards an MFA. Kinnell offered to let me audit. I joined a weekly poets' salon.

I got sidetracked. Off-Off Broadway, independent film. Then life.

Lost my voice and many other things along the way.

I'm working to find what I misplaced.

We leave our refuge to visit old haunts, longtime friends, book a New York City hotel near the Financial District. We bring the dog.

Our president's gilded palaces are surrounded by military. Dry fountains at the Unisphere. A heavy police presence. The dog parks are closed.

"You're talking like a geezer," Fawn says.

I *was* acting the travel guide to my memory, the landscape of a younger me.

Milo stays on his phone. Is he overwhelmed by *his* memories or just incurious?

What is he looking for?

"You can't park there."

We look to see where this voice is coming from.

"Where are you?" I ask the empty street. The building we're in front of has no windows, no entrance.

"You'll have to move on," the voice says after a pause.

We get in the car, do as told. Move on from what we later learn was the Federal Reserve Bank of New York, the holy grail of caper movies.

"Thank you," says the voice.

Breezes from the bay cool the 96-degree heat. Yachts dance. Kids kick balls.

"It was so quiet for so long," Trey, the widow of M., the man who was my best friend, says. "Now we're trying to figure out what comes next."

We've all known each other for decades. I saw Zora, Trey and M.'s daughter, held up at a hospital window within an hour of her birth.

"Nothing's going to be certain until after the election," Zora, now in her 20s, chimes in. "We've set systems to protect them, not us."

How would M. have reacted to this slow-moving year?

He wrote comics. Drew cartoons.

I hugged his widow and daughter longer than usual when we parted.

Something was amiss. I'd taken my father's widow out for lunch but passed on visiting their apartment. I stopped answering calls. Wasn't there one last thing I had to look at on my phone? Did I take my pills?

I scribble a note: "Great art recognizes the loss we carry. Or renders it so others can recognize a sense of loss within themselves."

"Where is *your* loss?" Fawn asks as I stare ahead, book open but unread before me.

I'm not sure I want to know. Though I am getting closer to being able to render it for others.

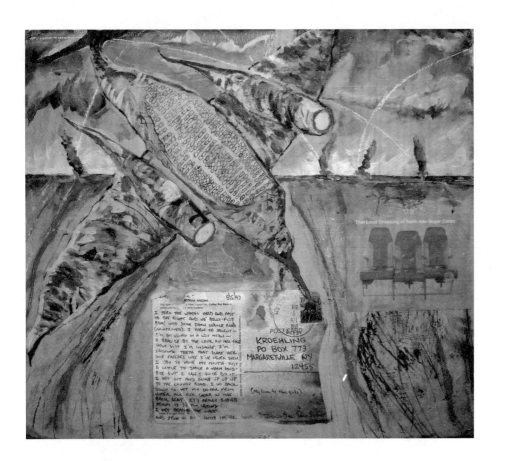

That Loud Gnashing of Teeth into Sugar Cones

SEDONA ARIZONA
This view of ... a from Copper top, Coffee Pot Rock is ... of west Sedona.

8/5/47

I JERK THE WHEEL HARD AND FAST
TO THE RIGHT AND WE BELLY-FLOP
BAM! INTO SOME DAMN SERVICE ROAD
(UNIMPROVED). I TURN TO JENNY —
I'M BUILDING IN A LOW MOAN —
I REALIZE BY THE LOOK ON HER FACE
HOW SURE I'M INSANE, I'M
SHOWING TEETH THAT SCARE HER,
SHE FREEZES LIKE I'VE NEVER SEEN.
I TRY TO MOVE MY MOUTH JUST
A LITTLE TO SMILE A WARM HELLO-
BYE BUT I CAN'T QUITE DO IT.
I GET OUT AND CLIMB UP UP UP
TO THE COUNTY ROAD. I GO BACK
DOWN TO GET MY GUITAR FROM
UNDER OUR BOX GEAR IN THE
BACK SEAT. IT'S NEARLY BURIED.
JENNY IS SO SIN CRYING.
I KEEP DOING WHAT I WANT
AND JERK IN R... ONTO THERE. LOVE, ...

POST CARD

KROEHLING
PO BOX 773
MARGARETVILLE NY
12455

(My love to the girls)

M. **said cartoonists** couldn't be edited. But I managed to fix his strips over the many decades we worked together. I, too, hated being edited.

I once went through a grueling back-and-forth on a piece about competitive would-be gurus. Rock-em sock-em swamis. After the sixth edit I sent back my original submission, and it ran, unchanged.

I prided myself on community publications that included unadulterated kids' voices and rants and pleas from the elderly. I kept their voices intact.

We used to be a nation of celebrated disparities, localized news stories, regional tastes. Dailies included classifieds and high school sports. Weeklies exploring how our home towns click. Magazines that digested what we needed to know from the news we should be digesting. All respected. An industry.

I've long liked working with speed, with a reliance on instinct. It's addictive. All doubts get tossed as you pile up deadlines. I thought myself a vessel, the work a gift. The entire process was a dance.

Now I worry about my latest discovery: The longer I work on a single piece, the lower my confidence in it sinks.

What happens if this Covid thing lasts more than a year?

Two men shoot each other's legs. Another two plug each other in the stomach. A pair of fourteen-year-olds end up in the ER with bullet wounds following a South End shouting match. An older man gets stabbed in the arm, then shot in the back. A seventeen-year-old dies in a rain of bullets at 3:15 a.m., just down the street from where I live.

"Guns are easy to get," says Jerome. "These kids shoot like in movies. They aim sideways, miss their target. It's a problem for bystanders."

A call comes in while we speak. Shots fired at the mall, only open for two days. Everyone fled by bus.

How do you afford a gun? "You don't need money if your attitude aligns," answers Jerome. "None of the safety valves—sports programs, school, the library, church, grandparents, parole officers—are available anymore."

I listen to a speech Jimmy Carter gave during the OPEC energy crisis.

99

"It is a crisis of confidence. It is a crisis that strikes at the very heart and soul and spirit of our national will," Carter said. He moved to the many ways in which we'd become a selfish nation, mesmerized by our wants. We'd drifted from a nation "proud of hard work, strong families, close-knit communities, and our faith in God," to a place where "too many of us now tend to worship self-indulgence and consumption.

"This is not a message of happiness or reassurance, but it is the truth and it is a warning," Carter concluded. "We are at a turning point in our history. There are two paths to choose. One is a path I've warned about tonight, the path that leads to fragmentation and self-interest. Down that road lies a mistaken idea of freedom, the right to grasp for ourselves some advantage over others. That path would be one of constant conflict between narrow interests ending in chaos and immobility. It is a certain route to failure."

Four months until the 2020 election and I'm already tired of it. Everything is now political.

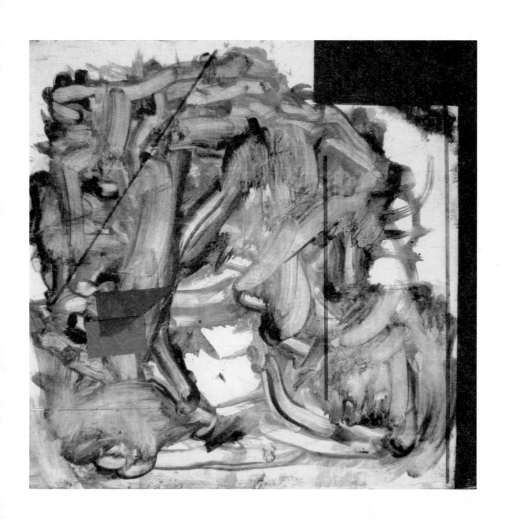

We rented a camp, took twelve teens.
Late that night they are stuttering tired
but can't shut up. I use my Dad voice.
"Keep it up and I drive us all home."

Is this education's future? Pods of kids from safe,
like-minded families?

I remember when our schools were finally integrated
in Virginia. Daily fights. Numchucks and click-clacks,
anything that could strike out at the other side. Then
a flurry of small, "religious," all-white schools opened.

One-third White, one-third Black, one-third
Latino; our group at WaWa is diverse. But it
has been engineered so. Not a bad thing but
one that needs to be acknowledged.

Camp's best as camp, a rare activity
one looks forward to for a few summers
then remembers for a lifetime, its hard
surfaces smoothed by fond recollections
of camaraderie and survival.

Buckets, pails and water balloons, masks and throw-away kazoos. Cheap fun, plastic treasure. Did you know that water pistols aren't available in 2020?

The teens speed talk. Biden versus Trump. Is Kanye crazy or just promoting? Dragonflies and flies and mosquitoes and ticks... Which were smarter?

"Who's the bigger threat, us or them?" I hear my son ask.

A wasp-like creature explores a bark-stripped porch rail in early-morning light, feeling every contour without touching. It flies an inch above the wood surface, disappears into a hole, then re-emerges. Skitters outside the hole. Re-enters.

I'm not interested in the science. I read in it a short story, a fable.

So many narratives now. Facts, alternate facts, fiction.

I watch my dog watch. She stares at the hole in the porch rail that the flying creature went into, then turns towards the water's edge. Something was rustling in the underbrush.

We need a narrative of narratives.

I run out of steam. My soul dives toward melancholy. Questions become threats. All edits and criticisms are shiv thrusts. The pandemic is a crisis because we don't know how to address death. Things have to change. We've complained enough. Could we be reaching an end to such dysfunction?

A kid hurts himself acting stupid. Tried a rolling dive off a moving truck. We are in the middle of woods;

I drive miles for a pharmacy where I find what I can to alleviate the pain from his swelling arm. Drive him two hours home.

I need *my* home, *my* own bed.

Rain starts to fall. It reminds me of southeast Alaska, where a heavy drizzle starts each September and doesn't stop until the first snow.

Catskills' rains on top of heavy snow: Major roads, rendered unpassable, crumble. Even the sturdiest of houses spring leaks or get torn from their foundations.

I have long loved sleeping through downpours, or settling into a comfy chair with a good book as windows cloud and streak. But I also feel a deep fear when the pitter-patter turns to downpour.

Biblical floods are real. And recurring.

The same for all scourges, Covid included.

My slide into diabetes was uneventful. I had trepidation when told I was pre-diabetic but the meds were easy. Better than the insulin shots I'd seen my dad and mother-in-law giving themselves, ashamedly.

I watched my diet, walked to and from the office. Stopped drinking due to medical interactions and looked over my relationship to alcohol, which both my parents used as a crutch. I contemplated what it could have become.

Covid hit. The weight kept coming. I stopped taking daily sugar counts. My doctor said everything looked okay but I felt the diabetes differently. I rewrote my will.

Would I do it all differently now, given the chance?

That's no longer a fair question.

Drinking stories. Family stories.

Talking my brother and me into a Puerto Vallarta nightclub for free. David insisting he'll pay. Falling over as he tries to explain himself.

My mother carrying her big glass of Pinot up three flights to our spare bedroom. After cocktails and a bottle with dinner.

Staying with dad for a month when his wife returned to Kyrgyzstan to memorialize her parents. Cooking for him, making certain his needs were met. And ensuring that he wouldn't drink more than the one martini a day that he said his doctors said was okay.

Memory in overdrive. I'm trying to find correlations. I don't want Covid to kill what little humor I have left.

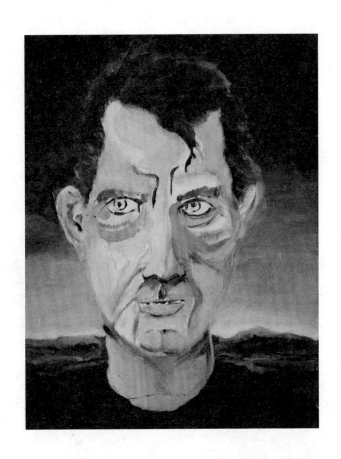

I **write a piece.** Randomly picked an event that resonated, had a bit of star power. Dinner with the Rolling Stones in Paris. I leave our table at La Coupole to pick up a French starlet. Return to find Mick (not yet a Sir) seated before my half-emptied plate of food.

"You ate my frites?"

"Weren't me, mate," he lied.

Then a second piece without ego or stars: My son, six, about to start school. We had a trip planned for an old friend's wedding. Something felt amiss.

"When was the last time you pooped?" I ask.

"Two weeks, I think," says Milo.

Shit explosion. A canceled trip.

In the third piece, which my editor hated, I defined "concomitance" as a conjunction, as two unrelated things occupying a similar space.

"My mind is the sole link," I wrote. "Juxtapositions exist within us all."

It's also the doctrine that maintains a Christian presence in both parts of the sacrament, taken singly or together. It's a base for holiness, a foundation for compassionate understanding.

Or maybe just hubris if summoned wrong.

I toss a toaster oven from the basement. I kept it 20 years.

Here's the story: I mentioned to Mom, living in Alaska, that my toaster died. She sent me hers, which I remembered from my childhood.

What tics am I passing on to *my* kid? Many worship canons of music, film, and literature. Will it all fade?

Milo says I'm obsessed with money, with keeping strict rules regarding time.

He's never liked toast.

I've had money since mom died. Wasn't expecting it or how it would change everything.

I used to keep an account of everything coming in and out, cash or credit. I obsessed about saving for Milo's education, maybe a year or two of "retirement."

I went through bankruptcy as we married. Fawn's request. Paid off student loans when I got flush. We fixed our roof, did a plumbing overhaul and upgraded other systems in the house.

As our financial advisor keeps telling us, we don't have spendthrift habits. We always bought lower after selling a home. We had no mortgage. We weren't obsessed with buying a pied-a-terre, a second home. No sports cars or big boats in our future.

I notice the way friends live, especially those on artsy paths. I ask about the way they handle their money and discover that wealth doesn't accumulate from work but ownership, and that we're all uncomfortable when the subject of money arises.

I still run numbers in my head, but they're more closely tied to dreams now.

Fawn and I have flourished enough on nothing I figure to survive if we fuck up.

Is the pandemic, like climate change and racism and inequality and corporate greed, becoming passé? Are we just accepting it now? I run the daily updates on our radio station, prefaced with ominous music. I check my news feeds several times an hour, as much for Covid developments as info on riots, political campaigns, the stock market.

Where is our laughter? What's funny now?

Everyone's talking about Jeffrey Epstein.
The man, like Keith Rainiere of NXIVM, had been characterized as the epitome of a "Me Too" target, a sociopathic example of the Me Generation.

It takes Herculean ego to reach such success. You rise well enough by following rules and pushing towards the best but to "take control" means leaping in with elbows out, taunts leveled, and other people's needs ignored.

Richard talks about the cult of death and its return.
"We've been hit with pandemic. It's still spreading," he says. "Even when we close this chapter with a vac-

cine or herd immunity there will be more. It's all a weird new take on that darkness explored throughout Central Europe in the first half of the last century," he said. "It's like the darkness that preceded the Renaissance."

That darkness has entered his drawings.

I reopen Michael Lesy's *Wisconsin Death Trip*. Explore Posada prints, Fuentes' fiction, and Mexico's Day of the Dead traditions. Recall all I can of times spent in India and what I learned there about lakhs and crores, big amounts related to the number of deities, the various levels and sorts of interpretation for any event or thing. The ways light and dark, fact and fiction, good and bad co-exist.

"Why bring up such darkness?" I ask Richard.

"To pass through it," he replies. "We don't always need to add to the hurt. The world supplies enough." We speak about readying our arms to finally embrace mortality. We agree to replay Leonard Cohen's "Take This Waltz," where "there's a shoulder where death comes to cry ... There's a tree where the doves go to die." There's a piece that was torn from the morning.

The son of Fawn's supervisor was twenty-five. He suffered from what his family suspected was severe mental illness, likely schizophrenia. They couldn't get him diagnosed. He'd end up in the hospital but was always released right away. There were no shrink appointments.

The young man stabbed himself repeatedly with a kitchen knife until he was dead.

Fawn reads me friends' fears from her social media sites. Covid. Trump. Democrats. Corporations. Opioids. Closed schools. Zoom.

Republicans. Litanies of complaint, more examples of fragmentation. As if the 20th century hadn't provided enough already. Our damned Human Condition.

I left Facebook loudly. I left Instagram because it, too, was naught but a repository of ego-flogging coolness. I didn't like seeing my likes and dislikes as a salable commodity.

I know what they want. Is that what I want? Were there happier days, before it all grew so complicated? Days when we seemed to have the time to tackle complex ideas, simple tasks, chores. I ply such memories, hoping to trigger my ability to recognize such moments now.

Here's another: I'm alone at the Cemetery House. There's a massive evening downpour. I take off my clothes, head into the rain. I run through the gravestones. I roll in the wild thyme.

I jump in my car, a suicide-door Lincoln. Roar across SR 42 and up the back roads of Beech Hill butt naked.

I feel a frightened thrill for the ten minutes I'm out. Like driving with the headlights off on a moon-full night.

I come home to a wide-eyed dog and cats, staring me down like the renegade I feel myself to be. I run a hot bath, listen to Strauss.

I think back to this whenever I open a bag of fresh thyme. I relish the body rush.

Memories are us.

Milo is getting ready to enter high school. There are Zoom calls about the rules he'll need to follow. They're calling the new norm a "hybrid": some days online, some days in school.

"I hate it all," Milo says. "Let me be."

My nephews drive to Mississippi. Everett has to get back to college and took his brother for company. His family insisted the boys stop using public transportation, living in dorms, or eating in dining halls or restaurants.

Per their mother's orders, they take shifts driving, eat from a cooler with mom-packed food.

My wife and I take the dog for a drive through a former hometown. We pass a friend of thirty years walking on a side road. Stop to talk. Coldness. An abrupt "I'll call you."

Covid, again.

A restaurant opens down the street. We walk down as a family. Eye the three other tables of folks as they eye us. Then the place closes.

More shootings around town. Endless protests about masks and lockdowns. Political convention count-downs. The meanness grows.

We want to go abroad next year.

I sit in the library, mask and gloves on per new regulations. We look out on the unprotected. A few stop to ask questions about reopening.

"We can get you books and DVDs or CDs only if you order them online," I answer through glass.

"But we can't get online. We need bus cards and copies. We have to fax in new rental agreements so we don't get evicted."

"Sorry, but it's not safe for us to reopen for such things yet," I answer, reading from a script.

Brayden Harrington, thirteen, speaks about Joe Biden on the final night of the Democratic National Convention. The young man talks about how the presidential candidate offered him tips for overcoming a stutter.

I had years of speech therapy. I know what it feels like to be teased and rendered moot by self-consciousness.

I was seated in dark rooms wearing giant earphones, asked to raise a hand whenever I heard a sound. My mouth and tongue were probed until I gagged. I thought that would be my life.

I took drama classes in high school. Endless "sound and motion" improvisational games. Waltzing while

doing word repetitions. My lisp disappeared. I started
using words with R's.

At my 20th high-school reunion, classmates asked how I changed.
"I reinvented myself," I answered. "Several times."

Hearing Biden and the thirteen-year-old, I recognize a crossroads
I had never thought to stop at. I could have held my challenges up,
touted my accomplishment, created a political career.
Instead, I embraced the world that shunned me and left it at that.

What do I carry from those thirteen years of lisping, stammers, no
Rs? My mom and dad never spoke of it. My sister doesn't remember.
Like having German measles or mumps, or bad colds and the flu
every year, some memories fade.

We rewash our masks in the sink. Buy a pack of new
ones every few weeks. Wash hands each hour. Hand
sanitizer's everywhere.
I never got tested. I figure that time will come. Did
I get this disease earlier, in the winter? Do I have antibodies?
Part of me wants to yell at my phone, at the television: Just accept things have changed. Death walks
among us! We fucked it all up but we can still enjoy life!

We are swagmen. Our memories Matildas. Waltzing to
keep the big rock candy mountain in view.

I **sensed other siblings.** Spent years eyeing family friends as possible brothers and sisters but it was only at forty that I learned about Harry. He's my only brother now.

My wife heard about an unknown sister at a cousins' reunion. She wanted to raise the subject with her father but the opportunity passed. After some research she found a woman living in the same town where Fawn's dad had attended college. The woman became family. Then blood tests revealed that Fawn's father was not her father.

No matter. Everyone decided family could be family without blood.

My sister insists that our mother, on her deathbed, alluded to a sibling we didn't know we had. I told my sister I wasn't interested in more family. The one Fawn and Milo and I had was enough.

Quentin texts me about the last time he saw his grand-mother several decades ago. She was deep into de-mentia, nearing her 100th birthday, and mistook him for her son, Q's father.

"I was so scared for you that entire year. I was sure you'd be one of the dead, Jerry," she said, teary-eyed, re-calling Kansas in 1918. The Spanish Flu. "Everyone was dying all around. No one knew what was happening."

That pandemic lasted from February, 1918 to April, 1920. It in-fected 500 million, about a third of the world's population at the time, in four back-to-back waves that ended up killing between 17 million and 50 million, and possibly many more. The flu surfaced at an Army base in Kansas, probably carried in from nearby farms, but gained its name because Spain was one of the sole neutral European nations reporting on world affairs during World War I.

The Spanish flu's physical attributes got the most mention: mahogany spots over the cheekbones which would turn a face blue, then black. Spontaneous bleeds from the nose and mouth.

"My father and grandfather survived the Spanish flu, but my granddad met a bad and dumb end a few months later," my friend says. His father's father, a court stenographer, read enough law to pass the bar. He was hired by a major law firm that moved him to Brooklyn and was going to send him to Cuba when it was discovered that he had a weak appendix. His New York doctors told him that should his appendix burst in Cuba, the doctors there would kill him. "They advised him to have it removed in New York. So he did, and it killed him."

"My grandmother was born in 1889 in a sod hut on the prairie. Her father dug a big hole in the ground and used the dirt for the walls. Her earliest memory was recovering from a fever that blew through, infecting her and killing her sister. She lay awake semi-feverish and heard her father talking to her mother in the other room. 'Why couldn't it have been Irene that died?' he said. Ninety years later I could tell she was still pissed about that, or rather deeply wounded."

Quentin and I text family stories: how my great-grandparents moved around Missouri for years, following great grandpa Fern's work as a blacksmith. The way Q's grandma was forced to move back from Brooklyn to live with family and all their household belongings were stolen.

I pull out Allen Ginsberg's *Collected Works.* I want to re-experience his songs of mortality.

He's one of many who could help us through. Summon whom we can, I write. Summon them all, so we can make it through to that flowering "AH!," as Ginsberg would inscribe his books during his late years, along with a drawn death's head surrounding those simple letters. Petals around a flower's body.

So close to Om. And Ha!

I reread Ted Roethke's poem about his papa's waltz. The one about a kid holding on to his drunken dad. I still feel it's one-two-three deep inside. At night as I struggle to sleep.

My wife shares the couch with our son, who stretches his feet onto his mother's lap. Berry, our dog, sprawls across both his people. Starky, who Milo still calls "the little one," bumps foreheads with me. CP creeps in and takes up her spot on the tapestry-covered footstool in our TV room's closed-up fireplace.

Meet Me in St. Louis. Szechuan take-out. Trash night chores completed.

A woman's voice rises from the street.

"Covid motherfucker loser."

"Lousy ass bitch." Mumblings, then a slammed car door.

"Another wonderful day in the neighborhood," sings our boy.

We all laugh, warmly.

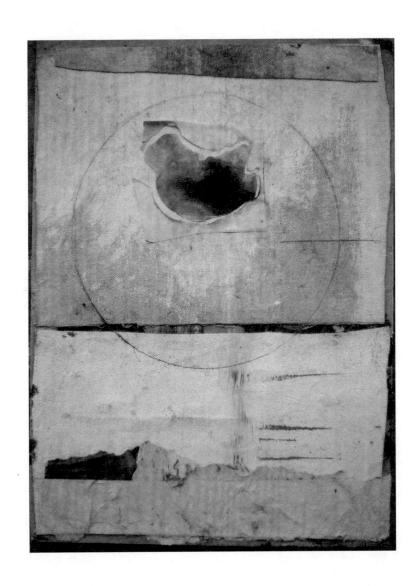

My back goes out. The computer freezes. None of the passwords I type in are recognized. I try to copy down the error signs that come up on my root screen.

My tech help is missing in action. The muscle relaxants fuzz the situation.

I just have to wait. Okay.

Life's a delicate balance of the technological and the magical.

One of my tech people is in the middle of Iowa, where the power's been provided by generators for a couple of weeks. Another is outside of Austin. A third is in Wisconsin, ready to move to Minnesota. Our server is somewhere near Phoenix.

The dog stares at me. I curse.

We walk up the hill towards Lincoln Park and the giant circular pool built there when FDR was governor.

We stand at the fence and watch kids frolic. Music plays.

The day's troubles recede. We head to a spot where I can let the dog run free.

As I bend down to unleash her, my back spasms. But it's nearing day's end. I figure we'll put everything together again tomorrow.

The dog and I get in the car. I need that driving form of thinking, where the front brain keeps me from crashing while the rest of me rummages. No notes. Music and a blurry landscape revealing possible signs for the future.

I've entered the final section of my life. Parents gone. Bereaved. Grieved other losses. Awaiting bigger change.

Three winter weeks in my darkened, high-ceilinged bedroom releasing phlegm. Mortality's shifting role in our lives fully contemplated. My Corona Angel. Scratchy masks and steamed spectacles. Making do with whatever brands of toilet paper we could find. A lost semester. Playstation friendships. Road lessons. Lonely library patrons, their public lives closed down.

A panoply of fears and anger. The hollow pop-pop of ghost guns on abandoned streets. George Floyd. The crucible of tear gas. My son's discovery how history works, at least in its first waves. The growing possibility of moving to Mexico.

Riots and counter-riots. An angry president. Political threats. Sorting good from bad. Joe Biden's stammer and memories of my own long-forgotten lisp. What will the GOP do for its convention, already moved twice?

Three seasons bled together. A dancing bear in the bathroom mirror.

The dog sits up as we move from cityscapes into forest. Fallow fields. She reaches out her paw to touch me. Wants a belly rub as we drive. Then a stop to run.

We've driven these roads in snow, floods, drought. Now plague.

Leaves are darkening. A whisper of fall. I try to get lost but keep recognizing landmarks as we reach higher ground.

Daniel Defoe made up much of his famous journal. Waltzing Matilda morphed from a complaint about employment practices and their effects into an anti-war plaint. Somehow, the dancing stopped.

I spot a pull-off. A rushing creek. No other cars. The dog makes a plaintive sound.

Refuge.

Covid was us, these months in 2020. But I still believe we are more.

Refuge, indeed.

From bereavement, forbearance. *Come a-waltzing, a-waltzing with me.*

Acknowledgements

The text in this work started life in the Woodstock Times / Hudson Valley One, edited by Geddy Sveikauskas and Brian Hollander. Early readings by Ed Breslin, Bruce McPherson and Will Nixon led to the commitment of our publishers to edit what had been a blog into what you now hold in your hands. Thanks to Sam Truitt for his publishing acumen and lyrical license. Kenneth Wapner, friend of many decades, pushed the manuscript beyond expectations into literary realms with guts and insight. Michael Ruby proofread, with brilliance and gentility. Quentin Hardy made the apt suggestion we should all adapt for our lives moving forward: lose all complaints. Wife Fawn Potash and son Milo Smart read, listened, and allowed for writing refuge trips outside of our home. Anja Aronska brought visual sophistication to what we dreamed of, and led us to our Toluca printers, Grafica Premier, who made this book what it is. Collaborator Richard Kroehling inspires me with his imagery, encourages me with his creative yearnings and achievements, and has kept my spirits alive through these strange times with insight and humor. The world, wherever we are, continues to engage.

© 2022 Paul Smart and Richard Kroehling

All rights reserved. Except for short passages for purposes
of review, no part of this book may be reproduced in any
form or by any means, electronic or mechanical, including
photocopying, recording, or by any information storage
and retrieval system, without permission in writing from
the publisher.

Published by Mountains and Rivers,
120 Station Hill Road, Barrytown, NY 12507

Mountains and Rivers is a publishing project of
the Institute for Publishing Arts, a not-for-profit,
tax-exempt organization [501(c)(3)].

Cover and interior design by Anja Aronska
Printed and bound by Grafica Premier, Mexico

ISBN: 978-1-58177-218-0
Library of Congress Control Number: 022939703

Barrytown, NY